"In the Lord I take refuge; how can you say to me, 'Flee like a bird to the mountains'?"
Psalm 11: 1

At the Foot of a Mountain

Poetry by Kevin J. McDaniel

Old Seventy Creek Press 2018

At the Foot of a Mountain

Published By:

2018 OLD SEVENTY CREEK FIRST EDITION

Printed in the United States of America

Published in the United States by:
Old Seventy Creel Press
Rudy Thomas, Editor & Publisher
P. O. Box 204
Albany, Kentucky 42602

ISBN-13: 978-0-9982374-7-3

ISBN-10: 0-9982374-7-7

About the front cover artist, Fred Thrasher

I was awe struck the first time I visited Fred Thrasher's home. He took me into the kitchen and we sat on opposite sides of the table. Behind Fred was a mural that covered the entire wall. It was a scene familiar to me, a Kentucky landscape with tall trees, native green vegetation, and a deer. At that point in Fred's life, he was a successful insurance salesman, the first person to take the insurance test and pass it without having a diploma or advanced degree.

Fred told me he was not an artist, but he had always been able to draw.

I was awe struck again when I visited the Santorini Akrotiri Excavations Archaeological sites and viewed the wall paintings of an artist or artist who painted pairs of gazelles on two or three walls, and painted a springtime fresco of lilies, swallows and lilies, and an antelope wall fresco.

What I saw, reminded me of Fred's mural. Fred had given up his career in insurance sales to pursue his art by the time I toured Akrotiri. He learned to paint in oils. He had learned to paint landscapes, natural scenes, and famous historical landmarks. Fred is a beloved Kentucky artist. His art like the frescos or murals in Akrotiri will be his mark on posterity.

Rudy Thomas, Editor Old Seventy Creek Press

Fred Thrasher's prints are available online or at:

Thrasher's Art, Phone: (615) 670-0648 or
Email:commthrash@yahoo.com

Thanks to the editors of the following publications for giving these poems a place to call home:

Broad River Review: "Gray Heron"— finalist for the Rash Award, 2018

Cloudbank: "When a Friend Falls in Love"

Common Ground Review: "Burnout"

Floyd County Moonshine: "Clint Eastwood in *Escape from Alcatraz*"

Free State Review: "Live Lobster"

GFT Press: "Newspaper Sailboat"

Gravel: "Down the road" and "Blessings of Country Living"

Sand Hills: "My Father's Lottery Ball"

Temenos: "When I hid death"

The Cape Rock: "Feeling Change Before the Fall"

The Heartland Review: "At the Foot of a Mountain"—finalist for the 2018 Joy Bale Boone Poetry Prize

The Main Street Rag: "Pink Sky"

The Paddock Review: "Oil Change"

The Pikeville Review: "Directions"

West Texas Literary Review: "Looking through Plath's *Mirror*"

What others say about Kevin J. McDaniel and his poetry:

The poems in Kevin McDaniel's *At the Foot of a Mountain*, are clearly written, detail rich, with intense endings, often unexpected. His themes, most important to me, are many: how age changes life's perceptions as well as the mirror image of oneself; how natural it seems to live on a country road with flora, fauna, and real neighbors, but even this joy doesn't remove you from the madness of a contemporary world with news of 49 dead and 58 wounded in Orlando.

Bill Brown, Writer of the Year 2011 by Tennessee Writers Alliance and Scholar at Bread Loaf, Elemental (3: A Taos Press, 2014) and Morning Window (Iris Press, 2017).

Kevin McDaniel's newest collection of poems hauls us on a journey along back roads, and interstates, sometimes in a traffic jam, sometimes pausing to inspect a wreck, burn a jalopy. Sometimes there's a side trip to home, or to the house that was home. And there's an intriguing blend of humor and seriousness, almost like road flares under water...playing, and working.

Clyde Kessler, a founding member of the Blue Ridge Discovery Center and regional editor for Virginia Birds, Fiddling at Midnight's Farmhouse (Cedar Creek Publishing, 2017).

With a keen and amused eye, Kevin McDaniel re-imagines his past and imagines his future, seeking the present of the poem as much for the making of it as for the stasis and peace it breathes. When caught in a traffic jam, he sees "fossilized couples" in "homes/ along the mountain's foot" (is this the projected fear of a young father?). Kevin's images imprint the reader.

Mary North, Winner of the VA Prize for Poetry, In the Tic Toc Cafe

Dedications

I thank fellow poets Parks Lanier, Jr. and Chelsea Adams for their feedback, which has helped this eaglet poet sprout wings.

Table of Contents

At the Foot of a Mountain

Down the road

For Robert Casto

where I played ball
   in high school,
I once caught a ride home
   after practice

in a red Suzuki Samurai
   where empty bags
of Red Man and snuff cans
   freckled the floorboard.

Coach C. told stories
   about West Virginia's dirt roads
that are *as windy and crooked*
   as Texas is flat.
.

He had a message
   for boys smoking pot,
spinning skid marks in the school parking lot,
   and racing to Three Gates (local dump)

to fight after practice:
   If they messed around
where I grew up,
   they'd be lying in a ditch somewhere.

He spat tobacco juice
   into an old pop bottle
while describing his family's
   ramshackle outhouse,

a father who drank too much.

and how the football field was a coliseum

where he could tear the head off
   all the crap in his life:

If you stand in shit long enough,
   you'll get some on you.
I interrupted with theories about
   UFOs, crop circles,

Elvis sightings in Kalamazoo,
   and how the U.S. government
covered up such sensational reports.
   The truth would be too much.

You're out there. You know that?
   As a kid, I had *real* stories,
but couldn't strip them down during a car ride
   to a moving moral

like a man
   who sees all the road,
doesn't filter his talk
   because it is what it is,

and there is no other reason
   to tell a story otherwise.

Blessings of Country Living

On my dirt road,
cool rainwater
fills in a pothole

where cardinals,
chickadees,
and baby blue jays bathe.

Good neighbors visit
to swap stories about struggling tomatoes,
a mysterious yellow squash growing

in the backyard,
the best spots
for building a fire pit,

or whether it's worthwhile
suffering sticky briars
for wild blackberries,

but I don't talk about
my nightmare,

General Grant plunging a shovel
through my chest because

I'm trying
to save
Vicksburg

as news outlets report
49 killed 58 wounded in Orlando shooting.

Feeling Change Before the Fall

The sun doesn't act
the same as in July or August
when it blisters the mower's arms
and leaves crimson welts
behind knee caps.

Its touch is gradual
like a lukewarm massage
with fingers pressing
up and down a spinal column
before patting the nape
of the neck.

We walk
meandering trails
under blue bellies
of billowy clouds
hastily draped over maples
showing premature yellows and browns
that we pause under
to visualize reds and oranges
that will come.

We prefer
they shower their drooping tapestries
down on us
at once
instead of one by one
since we, too, can feel
the blight that falls
on them.

Burnout

I'd like
to douse burnout
in kerosene,
stuff it
down
an antique
soda bottle,
and leave enough
for a flickering fuse.

I'd light it,
admiring
how fire licks up
the soaked accelerant,
before slamming it
through the front windshield
of a junkyard jalopy.

Flames
slowly eat
at the interior
before
the outer surface
is ablaze,
hissing & popping
seductive lyrics
as sirens do,
purification
of the archaic
down
to fertile
ground.

Looking through Plath's *Mirror*

"I am not cruel, only truthful—
The eye of a little god, four-cornered."
Sylvia Plath, "Mirror"

I don't see
a forgiving god,
but a reflection
of the man
I was back then
with hairs not retreating
to the bathroom sink,
a flushed face
without dark circles
or the birth
of crow's feet.
I look slender
from a side profile
in blue jeans sucking in
a trimmer gut.

I see
this former self
drowning
and swallowing hard
in view
of the mirror's
soothsaying attempts.
Wide eyes gaze back
like a thrashing river bass
whose lip is speared
by a barbed hook.
It's the catch fishermen
cast for and lie
about the most
or terribly forget.

At This Age

I.

At this age,
I am bewildered more
now
than when I graduated

from high school.
Back then, I rough sketched
decades
like a charismatic ball coach

who draws straight lines
on chalkboards, so players
see
pivotal plays.

II.

At this age,
I am harder up
today
than when I served chicken

at a seafood restaurant.
Back then, my daddy taught
me
to *balance what you spend*.

I saved
for muggy dorms with Victorian
windowpanes.
I catcalled bronze goddesses on walkways.

III.

At this age,
I am indebted to friendly
acquaintances
who gussy up counsel

in shorthand.
Back then, I put faith in no stranger's
messages
to tell me how to go.

I am a man
who diddle-daddles on his lawn,
wondering
where do cold headwinds end,

at this age.

Oil Change

Cars swarm archways
of the lube station
where the receptionist instructs
I pull beside the Nissan,
which I translate to mean
the big silver slug parked
behind the tiny blue.

She hands me
a paper
with a number stamped
in the corner,
so I can take my seat
in the crowded waiting area

alongside
a college kid working a Rubik's Cube
and a pregnant woman,
in green tank-top
and Daisy Dukes, bending over
to tell her toddler
be patient and wait
while the rest of us pretend
to be engrossed with Olympians jogging laps
on the mounted big screen.

Early that morning,
each driver drafted a shrewd plot
to avoid the rush, but fate
put us in
this purgatory
to learn
from mechanics

whose diagnostics show
we have more problems than a routine
oil change can fix
on a Friday.

Fellow Travelers

A shirtless fat man beats harsh rhythms
on his belly.

I walk my last lap. Grass clippings
obscure the path.

How fast must I go to torpedo
my tailbone?

When I pass by his park bench,
I throw up a hand.

He takes time from slapping sharp lyrics,
to nod approval.

How long until I sit to bare
my unclothed humility?

He throws a shirt over his back, shuffles
toward the parking lot.

I stretch before I drive like him
to who knows where.

Tiger
  languishes
in a cage
  inside my chest

where it sits
  dripping
in heavy chains
  not chuffing,

but bellowing
  songs
of melancholic rage
  and compulsion

to roam
  untamed
in my dark body
  cavity.

Tiger, tiger,
  beat boldly
so my mortal eye
  can see you rail against

shackled captivity.
  Do let your hunger burn
as hot as furnace flames
  through black jungles

in my extremities.
  But though I praise ferocity,
I will aspire
  to temper deadly ire.

Newspaper Sailboat

In a photograph,
I'm that guy
with cockeyed eyebrows,
an eye half shut,
and a straight mouth,
your poster child delinquent.
I'm in line at the grocery store,
bitching about politics
while the manager gets lost
checking prices for fabric softener,
or about the bag boy
who slides dish detergent
in with hamburger.
I mumble cuss
in the parking lot
because that other guy
driving the loud gas guzzler
parks over
the yellow line.

Late at night, I flip
through channels
before hitting
the mute button
to look over
and say:
spill your wad
of expectations
in a newspaper sailboat
made from yesterday.
Set it adrift
on a local river.
See an eddy wash it under.

Marvel at catfish spitting shards
of what's left. Turn around,
waltz weightless like Buzz
uphill to the car.

Lecture

For Taylor Caldwell

I'd like to sit
  in front of the class
with my head thrown back,
  drawing

on a fat stogie,
  mouthing smoke rings
like a classy Vegas act,
  and lecture

on the flavored varieties,
  how it's crucial
to buy slow-burning brands
  at a local tobacco store

to stave off encroachment
  of big-box bastards
and say *smoke slowly still,*
  make each one last,

to stretch out conversations
  you have
with yourself
  or a friend

who needs somebody
  to hear all that's going on.
Then have students brainstorm
  what warrants

such a holiday,
  discuss hypotheticals

like *what if an elephant*
  took a big dump
on your compact car

and you wait eons
  for a tow truck
as you sit denying the smell
  of hot stinking stench
like the brave few

who pounded
  one last cocktail chased by vintage Vermouth
and heard the band play
  one last song
on The Titanic?

Such is the reason
  to take a drag.

Clint Eastwood in *Escape from Alcatraz*
"Long is the way and hard, that out of Hell leads up to light."
John Milton, *Paradise Lost*

In a blue button-up,
reclined on a gray prison cot,
hands resting behind his head,
Eastwood studies lines
in the ceiling
like a passerby scrutinizing crowds
for friendly faces.

With a makeshift shank,
he chips cement blocks
under his cell sink,
not hurrying
like an inmate breaking out
of prison, but
piecemeal and patient,
exerting confidence
in a plan.

C'mon…
start throwing chunks
and get out
before guards catch on, dude!

Clint had me right
there
with him,
chiseling
not like a prying prisoner doped up
on caffeine contraband,
but like a mad sculptor
painstakingly attuned
to finer details

because it's hard escaping
to a place where
you're neither seen
nor heard from
ever again.

My Father's Lottery Ball

"It won't hurt you. It's just to kill plants.
It's called Agent Orange...and it won't bother humans."
Karl Marlantes, *Matterhorn*

Black barrels bearing orange stripes
in front of green military choppers,

a *PBS* Vietnam documentary,

makes me remember him telling how
he did what was necessary

to win

the government bureaucrats' unwinnable poor boys war.
He pissed venom on lush jungle tapestries and crops

in a futile attempt

to starve an unidentified enemy
who won the same numbered fate.

Both gulped deadly doses

of the orange poison
that he carried in life, limbs, and a depressed bloodstream

until his heart exploded, at home, in a chair.

The Other Man

I saw my mom
in the arms
of another man

in a black coat,
black pants with pleats,
black wingtips.

He had driven
in early pitch black
of a frigid night

to feel her tremble
in a blue house dress
and *her husband's* brown cap.

She hugged the man
after he had hung
an aluminum wreath

on the cold storm door.
She consoled me by embracing
a stranger's condolence

for her loss, *my daddy*,
who lay across town
in that man's warm funeral home.

Late into the night, we only heard
cold aluminum beating slowly,
slowly in the winter wind.

When I hid death

in a shoebox
I broke hard
ground
with a rusty shovel

The wooden handle
planted splinters in my
hands
I dug deep

where cardboard
now gives
rest
to a furry critter that

my little girl
thinks is forever in
quarantine
at the vet's office

I wonder what others
will tell her to
believe
when I am boxed up this way

Live Lobster

Like an orbiting satellite,
my daughter's yellow cap bobs

around the lobster holding tank
of the illuminated fresh seafood display.

He's not swimming, Daddy,
she informs me.

He's resting, baby,
I reply, thinking he's not alive,

but dead and destined
for a customer's dinner plate.

Depressed in an acrylic corner,
he accepts his fate like all lobsters before him,

rendered helpless with claw cuffs,
counting days until the tattooed cook in a dirty apron

salts and steams him in a scalding pot
that hardly muffles the squealing

behind closed doors of kitchens
in grocery stores and seafood restaurants.

For her, *he's resting; he'll swim later.*

When a Friend Falls in Love
For Becky Sherwood

When a friend falls
in love again,
at a class reunion where
her unrecognized ex flirts,

I'm the one
who becomes
a hot mess,
asking if she will

get rid of her Maine coons,
sell the house,
move clear across
the continental US,

burn diesel
and a bigger hole in the ozone
as she and her old ex,
reborn again,

crisscross the west coast
in a Winnebago
before hooking up
to water and sewage

at a state park,
which is all good since this is
her life,
a textbook example

illustrating
what was once thought lost
is only submerged
in her eyes.

Fallen Festival

Kids jump barefoot
in a gray bouncy house
that looks like a medieval castle.

Smaller children's fingers pluck
at blue cotton candy tufts
as they wait in line

to touch long, velvety ears
of a black Flemish Giant rabbit
who nervously nibbles timothy hay

or to hear a local farmer holler
in his raspy voice
the start of pony rides

around yellow taped-off rings
under brown and orange oak clusters
of the makeshift petting zoo

that is beside white tables
checkered with homemade novelties,
wooden scarecrows, clothespin wreaths

of The Flag, and Frankenstein fridge magnets
that cause *adult* peddlers and browsers
to waste time dickering over what is too little

or too much for painted popsicle sticks.

Pink Sky

When I paint
the sky on a canvas,
I dab the brush to intensify
a pink, bloated belly

because I want
more than
muted blue swirls,
more than

white, gray, curlicue clouds,
more than
a sagging, translucent moon
in a far corner.

I need a sky bursting with
fluorescent striations,
the kind that Grandma Arlene pointed to
during summer car rides.

Sugar, the pink is
God's throne shining through.
Always remember this.

And I do when
I speed
down a friendless highway
in late evenings

and see erratic red lightning on
a horizon
that is dramatic like
the naked man carrying his wife by pickaback

in Michelangelo's Flood.
I ache to go faster
as if in a high-speed odyssey
for the will-o'-the-wisp, to park where

the sky's seams split,
where fractured quartz slivers pelt my head,
and I, for once, can cry how good it feels
to be broken.

Clearing

Whoever lived here before me
    planted scarlet daylilies in strategic patches

and tucked lavender hosta blooms
    in shady spots under awnings,

but on one side of the house,
    unruly blackberry brambles compete

with Virginia creeper vines
    to choke out a lone cherry tree.

I try to salvage it by hacking
    at thorny palisade shoots clambering

up through the cherry's bushy crown.
    I lop entangled brush piles.

When I bend to break dead husks,
    a stray thorn catches a fatty part

of my nose, harvesting beads of blood.
    Good God, it is a hassle

to clean up another person's mess
    so that a cherry tree can grow unobstructed.

When I Hear a Hurricane's Name

A meteorologist taps the red swirl that spins
on a green weather map.

She reports wind speeds and historic rainfall,
calls the storm by its birth name.

I remember Hugo, Harvey, Isabel,
and callous Katrina,

aftermaths of disfigured signs, boats hung as trinkets
from entangled powerlines,

cars floated like pontoons, stranded holdouts
waved at FEMA helicopters.

I wonder if God sits down to watch winds
tongue lash beachfronts,

how long it takes angels to fill up gold stadium seats
from where they cheer legions

called to serve during catastrophes on earth.
I imagine my dead daddy

wearing a white hard hat in muddy floodwaters
of meandering cotton mouths.

He helps other long-gone souls ferry sobbing stayers
across overwhelmed streets of bedlam.

Gray Heron

A gray heron hunkers,
to the size
of a saw-whet owl,
beside my pond

to harpoon
a fat, orange fish.
His feathered form
retracts

like an accordion playing
a long note
as his wings slap
against rocks.

He raises his head
to unsheathe
a black bill that jabs
the air.

I bark and then
clang kitchen kettle lids.
He flaps clumsily
towards the house

on the hill
where he, undoubtedly,
snatches some of my neighbor's
smaller fish.

I wonder,
Do I tell him about
our long-legged pest,

or should I, like many others

living on our road,
only bother with what's mine
while he worries with
what's his?

In the morning,
the gray fiend visits
my pond again
to challenge me,

Put down your coffee cup!
Warn the poor man
of what's now flying in
his direction!

When I call,
my neighbor proclaims,
God bless you,
friend.

My heart feels
much better, only after
I respond
to a heron who tasked

my humanity.

Hotel Bathroom

During the tornado watch,
    we exhaust a night of vacation,

butt cheeks anchored to cold tiles.
    Digital nimbus clouds twirl on our phones.

I post play-by-play updates
    about a thunderous monsoon rioting

atop the roof and wayward winds
    sucker punching blue spruces and shrubs

that loiter along black creosote lots.
    The kids sleep swaddled in green onesies.

As the florescent light flickers above us,
    we occupy time with screwy conspiracies spun

on the evening news, gossipy anecdotes
    told by coworkers who sensationalize life,

and auspicious plans to move colossal clutter
    piled in our junk room that is part of every house.

When the rooftop next door flies off, I bargain,
    Dear God, I promise if you get us out of this

I will clean up my life, become a missionary,
    or at the very least donate debris to the Goodwill.

In a Jam, I See Prison Shanks

Traffic slows
to a slug's pace
today on slimy interstate,
tired truckers,
rush-hour workers,
and spit-balled school buses.
A digital sign blinks
news of a pileup.
Do I dare flip
on four-ways and hop
into the emergency lane?
Be my luck I'd get a postcard
with grainy aerial shots
of me reckless driving.
I'm old enough
to know it's futile to fret
what I can't control.
I distract myself
with commonplace homes
along the mountain's foot,
mile or two off the road.
I imagine fossilized couples
on creaky porch swings.
They sip sweet tea like communion wine.
Meandering ridges mirror
crosshatched lines under their eyes.
Serrated peaks are prison shanks
that gash the blue wigwam
as my car's stereo speaker rattles
stony background notes.

Directions

When a fellow traveler stops
to ask me
for directions to somewhere,
I don't give

simple street names,
routes with big-ticket turnpikes,
or how many turns to take
on the way.

I remember
the red barn on the hill
with brown baby goats grazing
in a field.

I remember
a yellow mobile home
where a bouquet of balloons is tied
to the mailbox out front.

I remember
the corroded blue El Camino
ditched on dead sedge
in somebody's yard.

I remember
a luminous cross at night
in the spooky cemetery on the left
before a flowering dogwood that overhangs

a metallic green sign for interstate.

At the Foot of a Mountain

In a reclusive cabin
where a wood stove hiccups
orange embers clothed
in gray ash coats,

the bottoms of my feet
feel bitter, raw air
circulating over every inch
of hard floor awash in

ghostly blue moonlight.
Through a window, I see
a lone yellow buckeye bend
in a boisterous wind

that makes me believe
it can bring down
the entire mountainside,
but I know spring

will come again on wings
of a gentler breeze that uplifts
saplings rooted sideways
in moonmilk underground.

About the Author

Kevin J. McDaniel grew up near Staunton, Virginia, in a ramshackle stucco home in Augusta County. Attending Riverheads High School, he played football, read poetry for the school's forensics team, and bagged groceries at the local Rack & Sack. In addition to his time teaching college composition, he has worked as a waiter, security guard, business owner, and freelance editor. He and his wife live in Pulaski, Virginia, with two daughters and a menagerie of pets. Throughout the year, they spend time in their beloved Gatlinburg, Tennessee.

His first chapbook, *Family Talks* (Finishing Line Press, 2017), draws from childhood memories. Other poems are rooted in experiences of his being a father, brother, nephew, and grandson. For his second collection, *At the Foot of a Mountain*, speakers wrestle with what feel like traumatic moments, moments (big or small) in a person's life when he or she believes an "entire mountainside" will come crashing down, as the speaker laments in the chapbook's title poem, "At the Foot of a Mountain." Nevertheless, by the end, readers are encouraged by the speaker's hope in a rebirth: "but I know spring/will come again on wings/of a gentler breeze that uplifts/saplings rooted sideways/in moonmilk underground."

*Photo by Michael Keyes of Photographic Dreams in Radford, Virginia.

Author photo on back cover, (atop Dragon's Tooth, near
Catawba, Virginia), taken by Erin McDaniel.

www.ingramcontent.com/pod-product-compliance
Lightning Source LLC
Chambersburg PA
CBHW031335040426
42443CB00005B/355